SALES NEVER GET BETTER
PEOPLE DO

52 PRINCIPLES
FOR SUCCESS

GARY O'SULLIVAN

Published by
Dorian Press
P.O. Box 770208
Winter Garden, FL 34777

Printed in the United States of America

ISBN 978-0615942919

DEDICATION

This book is dedicated to my friend,
business partner, and wife, Barrie.
Without her, this book would
never have come to life.

TABLE OF CONTENTS

ACKNOWLEDGEMENTS

Where do you start to give the gratitude due to the countless number of people who have taught you, enlightened you, and directed you? The one thing I do know is that whatever I am today, whatever I know, and whatever I have become is the sum total of the people who have intersected my life.

Perhaps Sir Isaac Newton said it best, "If I have seen further it's because I have stood on the shoulders of giants." To all who have allowed me to stand on their shoulders, I am grateful. From the great minds that left wisdom in their writings, the speakers from the platforms, and the one-on-one coaching and teaching I have been exposed to, thanks.

I would also like to thank Linda Gilden for her unwavering efforts in making sure what I said in this book was said correctly. To Chris Parker for his effort in the graphic design. To the great sales managers of America who looked at this material and gave me their insight and to the many friends who encouraged me, I offer my deepest thanks.

FORWARD

Not only do I teach people to sell, I too am a sales professional. Whether it has been working with a salesperson, a sales manager, or on my own sales performance I came to realize that trying to improve sales was not effective.

At some point it dawned on me that I couldn't improve my sales. Once the sale had been made you couldn't make it better. I came to realize that once the sales we made for the week or the month, there was no way to make them better. They were whatever they were. Yet, my goal was to improve my sales; to help improve the sales of others. The question haunted me, but how?

Then I came to realize, sales never get better, people do. It's only when the sales professional improves; it's then, and only then, that their sales will their improve. It's only when an individual discovers the principles of the sales process; comes to understand how to apply those principles, internalizes them and then acts on them do their sales improve.

Over the years I started to pay attention to the principles of thought and action that once discovered, understood, internalized, and acted on made people better. I wanted to know: What is it that some people know which allows them to succeed in the same markets were other people fail? What have they discovered and come to understand that seems to be hidden from others? What truths have they internalized that allow them to act when others seem paralyzed? What was it that others had discovered that allow them to ensure their sales were consistent, predictable, and repeatable?

In my quest I started searching for principles, primarily mental principles, that empowered people to give them the confidence and a sense of authority. I noticed that when I discovered a principle, a fundamental law it worked in many application.

I came to the conclusion that, principles didn't change; only technique and application did. Once I made that discovery, I developed a philosophy about principles and how they could serve to help people sell more consistently and to ensure that their sales outcomes were predictable and repeatable.

This book is a collection of the principles that had given me the mental muscle to keep going when I wanted to surrender, direction when I was confused, and allowed me to do what matters most every day. Having these principles simplified and internalized, I had the power to see the invisible and to do the impossible. I realized that if I practice these principles I would possess the power to be a more effective sales professional.

Once I started thinking about principles and power the possess I did little research. I come to understand that a principle is a fundamental law, it's a code of how things work. And that power was defined as the authority or the ability to act. It was from the basic truths that I developed a philosophy I now call PrinciplePower.

Here's a quick example to show us once we discover the principles we possess the power to do more, to be more effective, and do it faster. For thousands of years mankind tried to discover the principles of flight. It took about 2000 years until that historic flight by the Wright brothers for evidence to the fact that they had discovered the principles of flight.

Once we had discovered the principles we now possess the power to do things better and faster. It took us 2000 years to be able to fly about 100 feet. But once we had discovered the principles it only took a 68 years to fly a quarter of 1,000,000 miles to the moon. When we discovered the principles we possess the power, that is what I call PrinciplePower.

The purpose of this book is to share the PrinciplePower concept with you. So that you too, can learn not only from the principals contained in this book, but also give you the ability to discover other principles that have the power to transform you and help you get better.

Remember these three powerful concepts:

Principles don't change only technique and application do.

If you practice the principles you will possess the power.

Sales never get better, people do.

PRINCIPLE

1: a fundamental law
2: a code

POWER

1: authority
2. ability to act

PRINCIPLE POWER

The ability to discover, understand, |internalize, and act on the foundational principles which give you the power to achieve personal and professional success.

PSYCHOLOGY OF SALES

BELIEVING IN YOU IS THE FIRST STEP TO ACHIEVEMENT.

POSSESS THE POWER!

Belief is the strongest power a person can possess. For thousands of years the great philosophers have taught, "That which a person can believe they can achieve." Belief is the first of all qualifications for personal and professional success.

When you start to believe you will gain strength, courage, and the confidence needed to pursue your goals. It is belief that fuels the human spirit to look fear in the face and failure in the eyes and say, I will, I can, I must.

You must believe that in every challenge lies some secret to be learned, that in every difficulty that is overcome there is strength to be obtained, and in every failure encountered there is wisdom to be gained. Great accomplishment is only obtained after overcoming great difficulty. Great difficulties are only overcome by those who believe.

Remember: Believing is achieving.

PURPOSE GIVES YOU THE POWER TO PERSEVERE.

POSSESS THE POWER!

A clearly defined purpose is essential in helping you achieve your goals. Anything you set out to accomplish in the sales process will require you to deal with failures, disappointments and setbacks. Being able to overcome these challenges requires a clearly defined purpose. It is your "why!"

Whether it is your service to others or the things you are trying to achieve in your personal life, knowing "why" you are doing it gives you the power to persevere.

Remember: When you have the why you will find the how.

CONFUSED PEOPLE
DO NOT ACT.

POSSESS THE POWER!

Having a clear focus of what you want to accomplish is required for your success. Without a clearly defined objective of what you want to accomplish, you don't know what to do. The things you do will be busy work, not productive effort. When you have a specific objective and know why it needs to be done, you then develop the needed vision to get you into action.

Remember: You must act to accomplish.

DESIRE IS NOT ENOUGH, DISCIPLINE IS REQUIRED.

POSSESS THE POWER!

Most everyone has the desire to make more sales or to make more money. But desire alone is not enough. To succeed in sales, or in life, you must do what you need to do, when you need to do it, the way it needs to be done, for as long as it takes to succeed. This type of focused and consistent mental effort requires discipline: discipline to say no to ineffective activities and unproductive conversations and discipline to say yes to the thoughts and actions that lead you to success. Your thought process must be disciplined.

Remember: Disciplined thought leads to disciplined action.

MOTIVATION DOESN'T LAST; IT REQUIRES REPLENISHING.

POSSESS THE POWER!

Motivation comes from many different sources. You may be motivated as a result of making a difficult sale, reading a mind opening book, or by a positive comment. When you are motivated you feel, you believe, and you act as if you can accomplish your most aggressive goals.

Too often rejections, setbacks, and failure dilute or eliminate your motivation. Therefore, it is important to remember motivation does not last. It needs to be replenished. Read the right materials, listen to positive recordings and associate with people who uplift and encourage you.

Remember: Staying positive or reverting to negative; the choice is yours.

PRACTICE THE PRINCIPLE

SALES IS A HABIT.

POSSESS THE POWER!

Habits that we create become what we do every day. Sales, like any profession, has a requirement of things that must be done on a daily basis to insure consistency. This is accomplished through habit. Planning every day is a habit. Prospecting every day is a habit. Reading positive material consistently is a habit. Making presentations every day is a habit. Successful sales people form the habits of doing the things that must be done. Then and only then can they act in a manner that allows them to be effective everyday.

Remember: Our habits make us.

WHAT YOU FOCUS ON DETERMINES YOUR FUTURE.

POSSESS THE POWER!

Being focused empowers you to ward off distraction and move in a straight line toward your goals. The ability to stay focused allows you to make better decisions, more accurate choices and to take more positive action that leads you to your desired accomplishments.

To succeed in life or business you must focus on what matters most. Focus on the goals you ardently desire. Determine what needs to be done and commit to the tasks at hand.

Remember: Focus.

OUR THOUGHTS
DESIGN OUR LIVES.

POSSESS THE POWER!

How you think determines the choices you make. The choices you make determine the action you take. The actions you take determine what you become. Therefore, your thoughts create your realities. If you think about the right things, make the right choices and act in the right manner you will get the positive results that you desire. How you perceive things through your thoughts will determine what you make of your life, personally and professionally.

Remember: It is not how things look, but how you look at things.

WORK THROUGH THE FEAR.

POSSESS THE POWER!

Everyone fears something. It has been said that courage is not the absence of fear, but merely the conquering of it. Most individuals, who accomplish things, are people who fear rejection, disappointment, or failure. However, they are people who continue to move forward and work in spite of the fear. Fear is a natural part of the success process. The power comes when you decide to work through it.

Remember: Courage is not the absence of fear but the conquering of it.

THE MOST IMPORTANT CONVERSATION YOU HAVE IS THE ONE YOU HAVE WITH YOURSELF.

POSSESS THE POWER!

How you talk to yourself has an impact on what you think. What you think has an impact on what you believe. What you believe has an impact on what you do, how long you will do it, and how well you will do it.

Talk positively and with confidence to yourself. Only say things that will cause you to try harder.

Memorize key phrases that will be motivating and encouraging. For example, "Do it now!" "I can overcome this challenge" or "I can do this."

You believe you more than you believe anyone else. The things you say you believe: positive or negative, encouraging or discouraging, good or bad.

Remember: Be aware of what you say to you.

PROFESSIONALISM IN SALES

SELLING WITH INTEGRITY GIVES YOU CONFIDENCE AND FREEDOM.

POSSESS THE POWER!

Integrity should be the foundational principle of a sales professional. Your values and personal beliefs drive your ability to act with integrity. Commitment to your values gives you the strength to choose between what is right and wrong.

Integrity is personal intent. It is motive. When you have the right motive you will do things the right way, for the right reason. When you know you have acted with integrity you have a feeling of freedom because you have nothing to remember about what you did. You know whatever you said was what you were supposed to say. Integrity gives you freedom.

Remember: Do the right thing.

SELLING IS A PROFESSION.

POSSESS THE POWER!

Many times sales people do not see themselves as professionals. Selling, like any other vocation, is a profession.

In the general sense a professional is one who is extremely skilled in a given field and is paid for their services. People who view themselves as professionals, view what they are doing as their life's work. They are committed to continuous improvement and life-long learning.

Remember: Once you start viewing yourself as a professional you will harness the power to sell for a life time.

PRACTICE THE PRINCIPLE

YOU ARE EMPLOYED BY THE PUBLIC.

POSSESS THE POWER!

In the dictionary, service is defined as "public employment." The main reason people buy a product or service is to fulfill a desire or need or to solve a problem. They buy from you because they see value in what you offer and how it will benefit them. Therefore, your customers are your employers. Staying focused to meet every changing demand of your customers will give you the power to stay gainfully employed.

Remember: It's the public who pays the bills.

THE MORE YOU ARE PERCEIVED AS A PROFESSIONAL, THE BETTER YOUR MESSAGE IS RECEIVED.

POSSESS THE POWER!

When your prospects perceive you as being professional, confident, and competent in the knowledge of your profession, the better the message is received. When your prospects have a high level of trust in your abilities they are more willing to listen to you. Being perceived as a professional relates not only to your appearance, approach and communication skills but to every aspect of your interaction with others. You must know your product and service. You must plan well. Be prepared and punctual for client meetings. The more competent and professional you are the more comfortable people will be in buying your ideas.

Remember: Professionalism pays.

YOU ARE KNOWN TO THE WORLD BY WHAT YOU SAY AND WHAT YOU DO.

POSSESS THE POWER!

The only way you can show the world what your beliefs, commitments and desires are is by what you say and the things you do. The key words to remember are say and do. The words you use and how you use them starts the relationship process with your prospects, clients, and or customers. What you do about what you say completes the pictures of words and deed. Doing what you said when and how you promised forms the world's perception of you. This is a matter of integrity.

Remember: Say and do, that's how they know.

PLANNING FOR SUCCESS TAKES TIME.

Failing to plan is planning to fail. This rings true because failing to set a plan truly does set you up to fail. Just as a game plan is required to win in sports, just as a strategic plan is required for a business to succeed, so is a plan required for success in sales.

Spending ten to fifteen minutes a day developing a plan is a fundamental aspect of the sales process. To create a plan you must think about what you need to accomplish everyday to move closer to your goals. Planning helps you focus on the activities that matter most and think through the challenges you may encounter and be better prepared.

Remember: Make a plan.

GREAT YEARS ARE MADE UP OF GREAT DAYS.

POSSESS THE **POWER!**

Setting long-range goals for a year, quarter, or even a month is very important in the sales process. But you can't have a great year, quarter, month or even week unless you first have a great day.

Too often long-term goals give you too much comfort. If you aren't effective today or don't perform your best it is okay. After all, you have the entire year. No you don't! You just lost a day that could have turned an average year into an exceptional one.

Remember: Determine what you need to do today to have a great year.

MAKING A SALE
IS NOT ABOUT YOU.

POSSESS THE POWER!

Your customers don't care about what you want or need. They care about one thing only – a solution to their problem. They want someone who can meet their needs, offer a solution to their problem, or improve their situation. They want that process carried out in an ethical, caring, and professional manner. Selling is all about the customer and not about you.

Remember: Your needs only get met when you first meet the needs of the customer.

GOALS COME BEFORE PLANS.

POSSESS THE POWER!

Without a goal it is impossible to plan your day, week, and month. To make a plan you must be planning to achieve some long term objective. Therefore, you must have a goal.

No day should stand alone. It should be part of your master plan. Just as in building a house every day the things that are done are part of the blueprint, the goal, of what is to be created. Your sales career is no different.

The goal setting process is a powerful tool to help you create the blueprint of what you want to create. Just as the builder of a house would never start a project without a blueprint of what the end result was to be, neither should we start our year, month, or week. It is our blueprint, our goal that gives us the information we need to design our day. A well thought out goal gives us the detail to plan an effective day.

Remember: A goal is the first step toward a well-executed plan.

THE MORE DETERMINED YOU BECOME, THE MORE LIKELY YOU ARE TO SUCCEED.

POSSESS THE POWER!

When you make a commitment and are determined to succeed, you usually do. Failure has never kept anyone from success; not trying again to succeed has. Lack of knowledge never stopped anyone from succeeding; learning has. Fear has never closed the door to success; not working through the fear has.

To keep trying in the face of defeat takes courage. To discover what you need to know and to work through the fear requires determination. Staying committed to your goal will make you more determined. A sales professional who is determined to reach his or her career goal will not get side-tracked by less important things.

The more time, energy, and effort you invest, the harder it is to give up.

Remember: Determination is a key ingredient to success.

PROSPECTING FOR SALES

EVERY DAY YOU DON'T PROSPECT, THE NEXT DAY YOU MUST SETTLE FOR A LESSER DEGREE OF PERFORMANCE.

POSSESS THE POWER!

Prospecting must become a habit and a scheduled part of every day. It is important to add to your prospect base every day, because every day your prospect list is being depleted. Every day you want to have more people to talk to than you did the day before.

You are in the people business. The more people you contact the more chance you have to acquire new business. Being able to perform in the selling profession, in a large part, is subject to the number of people you have active in your prospecting reserves. By prospecting every day you ensure that the next day you will have a greater degree of performance.

Remember: Every day: prospect and profit.

INCREASE YOUR REJECTION; INCREASE YOUR SALES.

POSSESS THE POWER!

Rejection is an active part of the selling process. You must remember the more rejection you face, the more opportunity you will have to make sales, increase your income and build your future. Increasing the amount of rejection means you have to keep going in the face of disappointment and frustration. The power to increase your sales starts with encountering more rejection. The sales professional who experiences the most rejection also makes the most sales.

Remember: View rejection as part of the sales process.

REGRET LASTS LONGER THAN THE FEAR OF RISK.

POSSESS THE POWER!

Some of the things we have to do in selling require taking a risk. It is a risk to ask for an appointment, because you may get rejected. It is a risk to call on the biggest account or the most important person. It is a risk to try a new direction.

It is a risk to...do many things in life, but the fear of taking a risk is temporary, where the feelings of regret are long lasting. The thoughts of if only I had tried, if only I had made one more call, one more attempt, have a greater negative impact than dealing with the short term phase of the fear of taking the risk.

Success requires reasonable risk: pushing ourselves, trying new things, and going places we have never been. As uncomfortable as the fear of risk can be, it wanes in comparison to the lasting aspects of regret.

Remember: It is good to say I did.

A NEXT MENTALITY ALLOWS YOU TO ACCOMPLISH MORE.

POSSESS THE POWER!

You must develop a *next* mentality to help you keep going in the face of disappointment. This is accomplished by believing you will get a new prospect with the *next* call, you will get an appointment with the *next* contact, and you will make a sale on the *next* presentation.

Regardless of what happens, you must say to yourself, it will be the *next* one. Over time whatever you are trying to accomplish, if you will keep going, it will eventually be the *next* one.

Remember: Believe in the next one.

CHALLENGES ARE GOOD.

POSSESS THE POWER!

In the sales process you are paid to deal with challenges. It is a challenge to overcome rejection. It is a challenge to constantly find new prospects. It is a challenge to plan your day effectively. It is a challenge to stay positive in the face of disappointment. It is challenge to close the sale. It is a challenge to be organized. Mastering these challenges allows you to be successful. You should get excited about these challenges knowing the greater the challenge the greater the reward. To get the rewards you must overcome the challenges that cause others to fail.

Remember: Challenges create your opportunities.

NETWORKING REQUIRES WORKING TO CATCH PROSPECTS IN YOUR NET.

POSSESS THE POWER!

Net*working* can be a great source of prospecting and lead development. It is important, however, to remember at business functions it is not Net*visiting*, it is not Net*eating*, it is Net*working*.

Becoming effective at Net*working* requires planning and focus.

When determining which Net*working* opportunities to attend, think about who will be there. Once you decide where to go, plan how you will work the room. How much time will you spend with the people you know? How much time will you spend developing new relationships? Focus on the reason you are there, to get new people into your network.

Remember: The word is Networking!

DO THE THINGS YOU DON'T LIKE TO DO.

POSSESS THE POWER!

There is no career path that doesn't require a person to do things he or she may not like to do. Certain things are required elements in the success process; they must be done. Sales people do not like to do some of the things required to succeed; therefore they fail at the sales process.

One classic example would be prospecting on a consistent basis. Because of the frequent rejection prospecting is an easy thing not to do. To succeed in sales you must do the things that you don't like to do.

Remember: The power comes from doing.*6*

DON'T MAKE EXCUSES, JUST GET RESULTS.

There are always eager excuses waiting to be offered up. Don't use them. It is easy to find an excuse rather than a solution. It is easier to say why you didn't, than to share how you did. If there is a challenge to the sales process, there is a solution. Have the will and determination to find the difference between making excuses and getting results.

Rather than having to explain why you didn't go prospecting today, be able to tell yourself why you did and what you accomplished.

Remember: Focus on the solution.

IT'S NOT JUST WHO YOU KNOW, BUT IT'S ALSO WHO KNOWS YOU.

POSSESS THE POWER!

It's important to know people in your marketplace. It is critical in today's world to develop and maintain a database of some type to manage your prospects. This will help you maintain relationships and stay in touch with potential prospects and your current client base.

Yet, as important as it is for you to know people, it is also important for people to know you. People need to know who you are, what you do, and know where you are. Over time you can position yourself in your community to be the person people think of when they think of the products and services you represent.

It is important to your future to determine the most effective and appropriate ways for you to do this. Position yourself as an authority on a subject related to what you do; become a much in demand speaker to local groups. For people to call or recommend you, they must know who you are.

Remember: Who knows you matters.

PROSPECTING IS THE BEGINNING OF EVERYTHING.

POSSESS THE POWER!

The profession of selling has many elements that are important to sales success. Yet if there is one element that is the greatest of all, it is prospecting.

Many people who are excellent at making presentations fail because they had no one to present to; many people with vast product knowledge have fallen short because they lacked enough people to share their information with.

Many sale people think that those who are the master closes are the top performers. Not so, unless they have people to close. As important as skills, competencies, and knowledge is, without the ability to prospect effectively, build relationships and to have new people to see on an on going basis, you never get to put into practice what you know.

Remember: Without people to see, nothing else matters

PRESENTATION FOR SALES

YOU START CLOSING A SALE AT "HELLO."

POSSESS THE POWER!

Closing happens throughout the sales process. The prospect needs to buy into the ideas and concepts you are presenting at each stage of your presentation. Selling is a series of small presentations and closes that start when you meet your prospect.

Minor decisions throughout the sales process eliminate the feeling of making one big decision at the end. If the prospect has been making minor decisions about the different aspects of how your products and/or services will benefit them, the decisions to own it should be a natural part of the process.

Remember: Closing is a process; not something that happens at the end.

TELLING THE TRUTH MAY COST YOU A SALE; TELLING A LIE WILL COST YOU YOUR CREDIBILITY.

POSSESS THE **POWER!**

Being a person of integrity should be the foundation of every sales professional's career. One of the key elements of integrity is to always tell the truth.

Your customers deserve the truth, your company demands it, and it is just simply the right thing to do.

You may be asked a question and when you give the correct answer it may cost you the sale. For example, if your customer asks for something that you know your company cannot deliver (i.e. color, time frame, availability) you must tell the truth.

Telling the truth obviously doesn't always cost you the sale, but when you do and it does, keep in mind, the answer is the answer, the truth is the truth. Always be honest in your dealings with prospects. You may lose a sale, but you will never lose your credibility. By keeping your credibility you'll always get more sales.

Remember: You can always get another sale; you may not be able to recover lost credibility.

IT'S ALWAYS HARD
IN THE MIDDLE.

POSSESS THE POWER!

When you set a goal or embark on a new journey you may find yourself at a difficult place about half way there. If you aren't making the progress you thought you would, you can get discouraged.

Discouragement comes because you don't have the same level of excitement you had when you started and the end is not yet in sight. You must stay mentally strong. Remind yourself of the benefits you will gain by reaching your goal. Believe in the fact that you can and will find the answers you need.

Remember: The power to keep going when your are in the middle comes from your commitment to succeed and your refusal to fail.

YOU HAVEN'T REACHED YOUR POTENTIAL...YET.

POSSESS THE POWER!

Potential is an exciting word when it comes to your success. All you know at any given time is what you have accomplished, not what you are capable of achieving. What you don't know is what you haven't learned. What you don't know is what new skills or competencies you are yet to develop. Your best sales day, week, month, quarter or year to date is just that... your best to date. It is not the best you are capable of. As you increase your knowledge and skills, you will improve your competencies. Eventually you will improve your performance which will allow you to achieve more.

Remember: Your potential is unlimited.

YOUR ATTITUDE IS A SELECTED THOUGHT PROCESS PUT INTO ACTION.

POSSESS THE POWER!

Your attitude, the positive or negative thought process of your mind, is the mental engine that drives your behavior. The only thing you have absolute control over is your mind, your thoughts, and your attitude. Your behavior is born first as a thought. The motivation of your thoughts creates your attitude. Your attitude creates the standards of what you do and how you do it. You demonstrate your attitude to others by what you do, how you do it, what you say, and how you say it. A major power source for building a relationship in the sales process is your attitude; that selected thought process that is manifest into action.

Remember: Your attitude determines your behavior.

THE MORE YOU LEARN, THE MORE YOU EARN.

POSSESS THE POWER!

The selling profession, as any profession, pays based on skill level. The higher the skill level, the greater the performance level. The higher the performance level the higher the sales level. The higher the sales level the higher the income level.

Sales skills are learned. Learning more requires a commitment on your part to seek out the people and knowledge you need to improve your current skill levels. Seek out mentors who can coach you. Read about your profession.

Remember: Knowledge, acted on, is power.

LISTEN WITH ALL OF YOUR SENSES.

POSSESS THE POWER!

Most sales people don't listen. They do most of the talking! When the prospect is talking they don't listen; they simply wait on their turn to talk. If you desire to meet people's needs, you must engage in active listening.

Active listening requires all of your senses to understand the prospect or customer's concerns. You must listen with your eyes to see the level of concern, with your ears to hear the words, and with your heart to hear the emotion behind the words. You learn what's important to your prospects when you are listening, not when you are talking.

Remember: If you will listen with all of your senses your prospects and customers will tell you how to sell them.

TELLING YOUR CUSTOMERS YOU HAVE NOTHING TO TELL THEM IS TELLING SOMETHING.

POSSESS THE POWER!

When you are working on a project, problem, pricing, etc. tell your customer when you will be back in touch.

At the appointed time if you discover things beyond your control are causing a delay, tell your customer. Otherwise, they don't know you are working on it! All they know is you are supposed to call today.

Even if you have nothing to tell your customers, call them. In doing so you are telling them their concerns are important.

Remember: Keep in touch with your customers even if you don't have any progress to report.

PEOPLE DON'T BUY WHAT IT IS — THEY BUY WHAT IT DOES.

POSSESS THE POWER!

People always buy the product of the product. In other words, they buy what the product or service does for them or how it makes them feel. If it solves a problem, they are buying the solution. If it brings them joy, comfort or peace, they are buying that feeling. Be sure you are selling what the customer wants.

Remember: Your customer is interested in the end result of what you are selling.

SERVICE SELLS.

POSSESS THE POWER!

The principle that service sells is based on this concept: the more service you provide, the more you sell. The service is to professionally, ethically, and caringly explain the benefits, and value your products and services provide to the marketplace. A sale should be the result of the proper service being rendered.

In all aspects of dealing with potential prospects or existing clients, the more ways you can find to be of service to them, the more power you will create in the relationship and the more sales you will eventually make!

Remember: The more you serve, the more you sell.

PERFORMANCE IN SALES

WHEN YOU ACHIEVE MORE YOU BECOME MORE.

POSSESS THE POWER!

Setting goals that stretch you and help you accomplish things you have never accomplished before is critical to your professional growth.

To reach new goals you must learn new skills, acquire new knowledge, and develop new habits. When you accomplish this you become a different person. As important as reaching your goals are, what you become may just be the greater benefit, because you can now reach even greater goals.

Remember: Once you become more you can accomplish more.

FAILURE IS YOUR TEACHER NOT YOUR JAILER.

POSSESS THE POWER!

Failure is part of the growth process. It can imprison you or give you the freedom to succeed. Failure affords an opportunity for learning. Failure is never final.

After experiencing failure, you can start over better educated and better informed. Learn to see failure as an opportunity to understand what doesn't work and lead you to the things that do.

Remember: Successful careers are built on the stepping stones of failure.

SOMETIMES IT'S BETTER TO KNOW THE RIGHT QUESTIONS THAN THE RIGHT ANSWERS.

POSSESS THE POWER!

Although it is important to have correct answers to your client's or prospect's concerns, many times it is more important to have the right question. Asking the right questions helps the prospects clarify their thinking and gives you insight into their concerns and the real issues that may be keeping them from making the decision. Asking appropriate questions allows you to direct the conversation. The right question will give you additional insight and direction on where to go next.

Remember: The right questions help lead you to the right answers.

PRACTICE THE PRINCIPLE

YOU EARN PEOPLE'S TRUST BEFORE YOU EARN THEIR MONEY.

POSSESS THE POWER!

Gaining the trust of your prospects is the first step in getting them to be receptive to your products and services. To gain their trust you must be a person of integrity and do the things that you say that you will do.

Gaining their trust is accomplished by focusing on their needs. The more comfortable the prospects get and the more confident they perceive you, the more their trust builds in you. Once they start to trust you their minds will open and they will listen to you.

Remember: It is only when prospects begin to trust you that they will be willing to buy from.

LOGIC GETS PEOPLE TO THINK; EMOTIONS GET PEOPLE TO ACT.

POSSESS THE POWER!

In the sales process logic is very important, yet it is through feelings and emotions that people act. Getting people to act is required to be successful in the sales process. This is only accomplished by getting people emotionally involved in your products and services. Logic explains the what, emotions explains the why. Logic tells them what it is, emotion explains what it does for them.

Remember: Logic tells; emotion sells.

OBJECTIONS KEEP THE SALES PROCESS MOVING.

POSSESS THE POWER!

Objections keep the conversation moving forward and give you insight into what your prospect is thinking. Objections allow you to deal with an issue and then move on to other aspects that eventually lead you to the sale. Your attitude toward objections will determine your response to them. If your attitude is that objections are a request for more information, you will welcome them. The better you become at dealing with the objections you get, the more sales you will make.

Remember: Objections can be a positive step toward a sale.

PEOPLE WHO SUCCEED, PLAN TO.

POSSESS THE POWER!

Success doesn't usually come as a surprise to successful people. The reason is simple; they planned to succeed. In planning for success you must decide what success is for you. Define what you need to do and then do it. Once you start, keep track of what is working and what is not. Make the needed changes and keep going.

Remember: Plan, practice, perfect.

MEASURE EVERYTHING.

POSSESS THE POWER!

You must have clearly defined standards as to what is acceptable for what you are trying to accomplish everyday. Creating a feedback system to indicate your success will help you. You should have standards of performance for the critical areas of your sales efforts and continuously strive to meet and exceed them. Only with well-defined standards can there be improvement.

Remember: Everything worthwhile can be simply defined and measured.

ACTIVITY LEADS TO ACCOMPLISHMENT.

POSSESS THE POWER!

Activity is required to obtain results. But it must be the right activity. There is always something you can do. Yet you must always be asking yourself, "Is what I am doing right now leading me to my goals?"

Selling is about accomplishment, getting results. Getting results requires activity. Yet you will only get the desired results if you are engaged in the right activities. Activity leads to accomplishment if the activity is correct.

Remember: Stay active doing the right things.

NUMBERS ARE YOUR FRIENDS.

POSSESS THE POWER!

Good sales people operate on good information. Accurate numbers are trusted friends that will give you what you need to operate and improve you sales efforts. Like good friends, there are two essential factors required: You must be truthful and you must stay in close contact. Being truthful means keeping an accurate account of the results of your efforts, all of the data from prospecting to closing. Review the data on a regular and ongoing basis to stay aware of what is working and what needs improving. This truthful exchange keeps the relationship strong.

Remember: Your friends will give you the power to succeed.

SELLING IS A PAID FOR PERFORMANCE PROFESSION.

POSSESS THE POWER!

We must remember that selling, like many other career paths, is a paid for performance profession. We get paid when we perform. It is not about talking a good job, it is about doing a good job.

Being able to get results in the free enterprise system is a skill that is highly sought after and well rewarded. The people who can deliver and do it on a consistent basis are the few, the professional, and the well paid.

Remember: Sales people are paid to get results.

BELIEVING IS NOT ENOUGH. KNOWING IS NOT ENOUGH. YOU MUST ACT.

POSSESS THE POWER!

Knowing the skills and competencies of your profession is not enough. As critical and important as it is, knowledge simply is not enough. You must act on what you know. You must use your skills and act on your competencies to accomplish you goals.

When you finish reading this book, you will have many important tools of a successful sales professional. They have been proven over the years. But if you put the book back on your bookshelf and do not apply what you have learned, the knowledge you have gained will not benefit you. It is what you do with what you know that matters.

Remember: A– Accumulate knowledge
C– Consider your options
T– Take action

For information on this or other
products, or for information regarding
Gary O'Sullivan's presentations,
call or write to:

Gary O'Sullivan
P.O. Box 770208
Winter Garden, FL 34777
407-877-8700
garyosullivan.com

Made in the USA
Columbia, SC
25 August 2022